Parent's Page

"...Have you considered, if your water were one morning to have seeped away, who then could bring you clear-flowing water?" (Qur'an 67:30).

The environment is a signpost of Ultimate Reality. In other words, the Earth and all of creation point us toward Allah (SWT). Verse upon verse in the noble Qur'an urges us to ponder on the environment as a means to cultivate awe, gratitude, and humility within ourselves.

However, while reflection is important as a first step, we must go a step further by putting this appreciation into action. We must care for the environment and strive to live responsibly because looking after the Earth is our duty as Muslims. In fact, Allah (SWT) says, "We offered the *amaanah* [trust, moral responsibility] unto the heavens and the earth and the hills but they shrank from bearing it and were afraid of it. And man assumed it" (Qur'an 33:72). Thus, we have an obligation of stewardship in order to care for all creation.

In this book, we share two lessons about the environment. The first lesson teaches that through spending time outdoors and by learning about the magnificence of creation, we are able to understand the attributes of God. We can see His "fingerprint" in everything that He creates. In our first story, "The Magnificent Maker," Asad and his friends explore the water system and discover that they can learn a lot about Allah (SWT) through what He has created.

Our second lesson communicates the harm in adopting the "free-rider" concept as it relates to the environment. That is, there is a tendency for us to assume that somebody else will take care of it. The reality is, though, that if we each don't play our part, we will all fail together. In our second story, "Somebody Else," Zaid misbehaves towards the environment until he realizes that each person's actions matter, and we must do whatever we can to help our world.

Credits & Honors
Art Director: Annie Idris
Editors: Amin Aaser & Sana Aaser
Researcher: Noori Bibi
Creative Developers: Saharish Arshad,
　　　　　　　　　　Maryum Mohsin,
　　　　　　　　　　& Amin Aaser

Asad is embarrassed.

"Oops, I wonder how that got programmed."

"No machine-making today, buddy. It's time to master the water cycle. Can you help us?"

"Well, it all starts with the sun."

"The sun heats up water in our lake. The water begins to evaporate."

THE WATER CYCLE

CONDENSATION
Evaporation turns into clouds and comes back to Earth through rain and snow.

EVAPORATION
Water evaporates into air because of sun

PRECIPITATION
Rain and snow goes into an underground aquifer, which feeds back into the lake and goes to water tower.

AQUIFER

LAKE CALHOUN

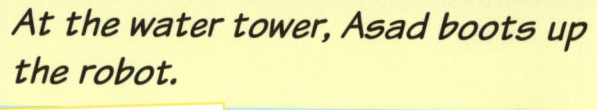

Questions:

1. What can we learn about Asad by the fact that he created Ali the Android?

2. What can we learn about Allah (SWT) by the way He created the water system?

3. When there is a water shortage or pollution, who do you think caused it?

Allah's (SWT) Perfect Mathematical Designs

ADD COLOR TO THIS PICTURE!

In the Qur'an

صُنْعَ ٱللَّهِ ٱلَّذِىٓ أَتْقَنَ كُلَّ شَىْءٍ

"(Such is) the artistry of Allah, who perfected all things."
(Surah An-Naml, Ayah 88)

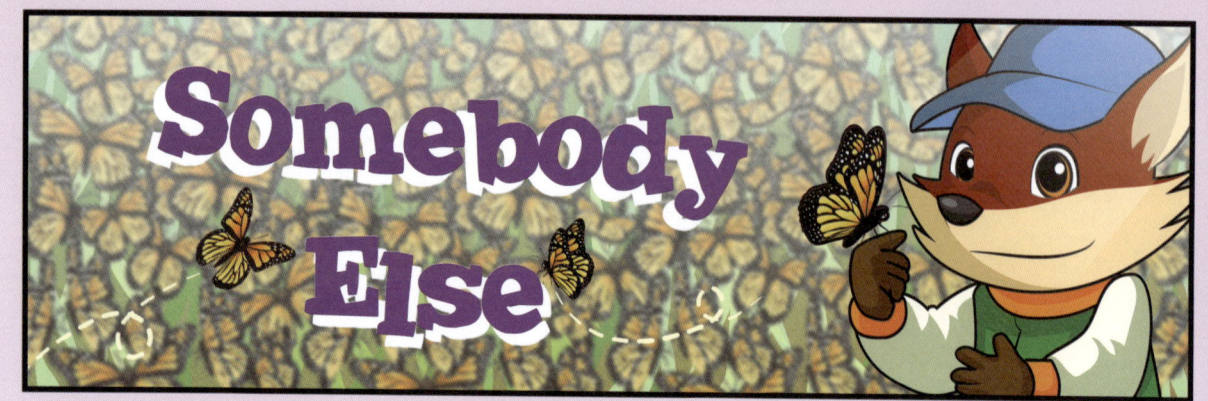

Somebody Else

The Maple Grove Islamic Center hosts its annual picnic at Lake Calhoun.

Let's go canoeing first.

Perfect! And then we can visit the monarch butterfly sanctuary.

The girls pass by Zaid eating a large bag of chips. Zaid yells over at them.

What's up, sistas!

Salaam, Zaid.

Questions:

1. Zaid said that one little butterfly doesn't matter. Is he wrong?

2. Whose problem is it?

3. Do the decisions and actions of one person actually matter?

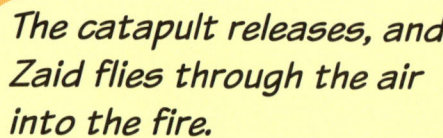

Islamic Inventions

CAN YOU SPOT the 10 differences?

In the 13th century, the scholar Abu al-Hasan (Alhazen) from Basra was the first person to describe how the eye works.

Abu al-Hasan carried out experiments with reflective materials. He found that curved glass surfaces could be used to make things appear larger.

His glass "reading stones" were the first magnifying glasses. It was from these that eyeglasses were later developed.